Singer Wanted

Written by
Rob Waring and **Maurice Jamall**

Before You Read

to sing a song

keyboard

to wear

music

clothes

pop music

drums

rock band

guitar

nervous

In the story

Jenny   Faye   Tyler   John   David   Daniela   Gemma

"Look, it's Faye's band," says Jenny. She is talking to her friend, Daniela.

Daniela says, "Yes, Faye's in the band, Hot Rock."

Faye is their friend. She plays the keyboard for Hot Rock.

Faye's band wants a new singer.

3

"Look, Jenny," says Daniela. "Hot Rock wants a new singer. I can join the band."
"That's a great idea! You're a really good singer, Daniela," says Jenny.
Daniela says, "I want to sing in Faye's band. I want to be Hot Rock's singer."

Their friend, Gemma comes to them. "What's this?" she asks.
Jenny tells Gemma about the band.
"Good. I want to sing for Hot Rock," says Gemma.
"Do you want to be in the band, Jenny?" Gemma asks.
Jenny smiles. She says, "No, but Daniela does."

It's Saturday. Today Hot Rock is looking for their new singer. John plays the guitar. Tyler plays the bass guitar, and David plays the drums. Faye plays the keyboard.

Jenny asks Daniela, "Are you okay?"

"No, not really," she says. "I'm really excited, but I'm very nervous. I'm not a good singer."

"Don't be nervous," says Jenny. "And don't worry. Everybody likes your singing."

Faye sees Daniela. She says, "Hi, Daniela. Do you want to be in the band?"

"Yes, I do," says Daniela. "But I'm really nervous."

Gemma comes into the room.

"Look, Gemma Walsh is here," Daniela says.

"She's a really good singer. I can't win now."

Daniela sings a song with the band. But she does not sing well. She is too nervous.

But Jenny likes Daniela's singing. Faye likes her singing, too. "Good job, Daniela!" she says.

"Don't say that," Daniela says. "I'm a really bad singer."

"No, you're not," says Jenny.

Gemma sings for the band, too. She sings very well.
Everybody loves her singing. She is a very good singer.
"She's very good!" thinks Jenny.
Daniela knows Gemma is very good, too.

The band talks about Gemma and Daniela.
David, John, and Tyler want Gemma. But Faye wants Daniela.
"I like Daniela's singing," says Faye.
"Yes, but Gemma is very, very good," says Tyler.
They talk for a long time.

Faye says, "We want Gemma to be the new singer!"
"Thank you, Faye. Thank you, everybody," Gemma says.
She is very happy.
"Congratulations, Gemma," says Daniela.
Daniela is very sad. But she is happy for Gemma.

Later, Daniela speaks to Jenny.

"I'm not a good singer. I'm really bad," she says.
"Gemma is a very good singer."

"Yes, she is. But Daniela, you are a good singer, *too*,"
says Jenny. "A very good singer." Jenny smiles at
Daniela.

"No, I'm not," Daniela says.

The next day, Gemma meets the band again.
"Hello, Gemma," says Tyler.
The band is happy with their new singer.
Everybody is very excited. Gemma is very excited, too.

Gemma gives some clothes to David and John.

"These clothes are for you," she says.

"But I don't want to wear these," David says. "I don't like them."

Gemma says, "And we have a new name for the band. It's on the clothes." It says 'Gemma and Hot Rock.'

"The band's name is 'Hot Rock', not 'Gemma and Hot Rock!'" says Faye. "We don't want a new name."

Gemma says, "Let's sing some pop songs."
Faye says, "I don't want to play pop music."
"But I want to play pop music," says Gemma. "And I'm the singer."
John says, "But we are a rock band. We are not a pop band."
"And this band is *everybody's* band, not yours," says Faye.

The next day Faye, Tyler, David, and John see Daniela.
"Daniela, we want you to be in our band," Faye says. "We want you to sing with us!"
"Me?" says Daniela. "Really?" she says. "Can I be in your band? But, what about Gemma?" she asks.
Faye says, "Gemma doesn't sing for us now."
"Thank you, thank you, thank you," says Daniela.